This is my story; this

Emma Majc_

All proceeds from the sale of this book are donated to:

The Miscarriage Association

17 Wentworth Terrace
Wakefield WF1 3QW

Registered Charity Number

1076829 (England & Wales),

SC039790 (Scotland)

First published in 2013.

ISBN: 978-1-300-69216-4

For Rachel

Contents

Foreword

An estimated one in four pregnancies ends in miscarriage, making it an experience shared by many women and their partners. Even so, this is often a hidden loss, a silent grief, where painful feelings remain unspoken. It can be a very frightening, distressing and lonely experience.

Emma Major has chosen to speak out. She shares poetry and prose that she has written over many years, words that express her feelings and words that have helped her to heal.

They are words from the heart, loud and true and a gift to others.

Ruth Bender Atik
National Director
The Miscarriage Association

Introduction.

This book is both my story and my song.
It is the story of my babies who died before they were born;
it is my song of healing and hope in grief, given as a gift to others.

It is not a diary or an autobiography of my experience; rather it is a collection of poems and prose which I have written over the years in memory of my four baby boys and in the journey of grief which I have travelled. They were written as a form of healing and they are given now in the hope that they might help the healing of those who read them.

I am a mum of angels;
We are many in number;
We are never alone.

Emma

I leave you with **a poem of thanks**.

Many people have helped me
In the journey to this book
To name them would take far too long
But one person needs my thanks
For my rock through every single thing
Through good days and the bad
Thank you Mike, for all you are
Especially being Rachel's brilliant dad.

This is my story; this is my song

This is my story of babies who died
This my story no more can I hide
This my story it shapes me each day
This my story it never goes away

This my song of hope for tomorrow
This is my song of joy from the sorrow
This is my song of comforting each other
This is my song knowing we're in it together

These are my words of truth and of pain
These are my words of emotion and strain
These are my words which each day help me cope
These are my words of love, peace and hope

1

Angels

An angel watches over us
Not alone, he's with his brothers
He knows he's loved and always was
I just wish I could have held him once

I knew that Angels were real enough
They're in the bible after all
But I never knew they could be made so soon
Or loved so much down here

Angels know that you are loved
This fact time won't take away
I love you as much today as then
That you know it is what I pray

Baby

Don't call my baby a fetus
An embryo or anything else
My baby was a baby
No matter how old he was
As soon as I knew I was pregnant
I had his life in sight
His birth and early weeks at home
The feeds and sleepless nights
I was a mum from that first day
In love with my baby boy
When he died I fell apart
No longer was there hope and joy
So don't tell me my baby boy
Was anything less than a baby to me
He deserves to be grieved and missed by us
Perhaps these tears will help you see

Compassion

Compassion wasn't really found
Inside the hospital
But once outside my friends were all
I needed then, and more

Making sure I'd time to grieve
Visiting and chatting
Not expecting anything much
Just allowing me to start healing

It seems hard to support a family
Whose baby died unexpected
Unless you know that all they need
Is compassion and love reflected

So please don't think you're not enough
That you can't help a friend in need
Because if you care and grieve with them
Then you're the friends they need indeed

Death

There are many one syllable words
Used to name the death of a baby
Like Loss, Miss and Still
Or Sleep, Fail and Weak

But one word could replace them all
One word that cuts straight to the point
One syllable, all powerful
Death

Death

My babies died
My babies are dead
Death is very real to me
I'm not afraid to name it

When other words are used
It doesn't disguise the truth
They don't make it any better
So please just speak of death

Empty

Empty arms,
Empty heart,
Empty cot,
Empty room,
Empty house,
Empty womb,
Empty family,
Empty life,
Empty.

Together we remember (Babyloss Awareness Day)

Every year we come together and we remember
We remember the babies who died before birth
In light
In tears
In love
In prayers
In our hearts
Together across the globe

Feelings

So many feelings
Stomping through my heart
Not taking trouble
To find out I'm falling apart

Some of them are happy
They make me feel much worse
How can I be happy
When I will never nurse

Most of them are sad
With tears chasing behind
Some of them are angry
Making my teeth grid

Some are confused
Can't even give them a name
Others I can't tell you
They're wrapped up in my shame

I'll tell you that I'm ok
That it's better day by day
But if you listen closely
You'll ignore what I say

My feelings still are stomping
Over everything I see
I hear that I'll recover
But right now please let me be.

Dear God

Dear God
Why did my baby have to die?
Why did you want him home?
Why couldn't he stay here with me?
Why do I have to moan?

Why can't you stop these babies dieing?
Is it too big to do?
Please don't tell me you let it happen;
That's not what I know about you!

Where is my baby now God?
What age is he there with you now?
Does he miss me too God?
Will I see him again, tell me how!

I wish you could hold my hand God
I need to feel your love here with me
Thankyou for loving my baby God
Please don't forget about me.

Hole

There's a hole in my heart
Where once there was you
It won't ever heal
No matter what I do

There's a hole in my life
Been there since you left me
It won't ever heal
No matter what else I see

There's a hole in my dreams
Where you used to play
It won't ever heal
Because you've gone away

There's a hole in our family
Where we thought there'd be two
But you're part of us still
Do you hear us pray with you?

Invisible

Invisible heartbeat
Invisible limbs
Invisible life
Invisible things

Invisible grief
Invisible pain
Invisible memories
Invisible strain

Invisible baby
Invisible remembrance
Invisible facts
Invisible experience

Jinxed

Am I jinxed?
It seems that I am
Once is bad luck
But by the fourth I feel damned

Perhaps I'm being punished
For mistakes in my past
But this it's too much
How long can this last?

I knew it used to happen
But never thought it could now
I know I'm not jinxed
I pray no one else thinks they are

Kendi

Miracle of Africa
Baby of hope
Hanging on in there
Not letting go
Called home by God
Not meant to be here
Broke my heart
Remembered everyday

Leof

Boy we never expected
Baby miracle
Hidden for too long
Not treated early enough
Couldn't hold on any more
Left a sister
Left us all
Loved one

Mummy

I am a mummy
A child calls me by that name
But being a mummy
Started long before that time

I became a mummy
As soon as I first knew
That there was a baby
Growing within me

When the midwives at each visit
Asked if I was a mum
I used to hesitate
Not knowing how to respond

Sometimes I'd say yes
Explaining what that meant
Usually I'd say no
Then I would lament

Because I knew what they were asking
But it was too cruel to see
Too cruel to think about
Too much to be me.

Never

Never did I imagine
I could survive such pain
Never did I imagine
I'd have to do it over again
Never did I imagine
The wait would be so long
Never did I imagine
I could be so strong
Never did I imagine
I'd have four children to miss
Never did I imagine
My life would be like this

I never met my boys

I never met my boys
Never shared their joys
But in me once they lay
And in my heart they stay

Options

Where do we go from here?
What are options for a family?
Do we stop or keep on trying?
What route will keep our sanity?

Some days another pregnancy
Seems to be the natural choice
Other days I just don't have
The energy, positivity or poise

I'm just too scared of what might be
Can't bear to take the risk
But if we never try again
There's no chance of getting the gift

Adoption is another route
That we might choose to follow
But are we ready to go for that?
Too many options to swallow

Eventually we took the plunge
We tried again once more
Thank you God for giving us strength
She makes us happy to our core

Prayer

Father God

Wherever Jesus went, children flocked to his side. He gathered them to him and included them in his loving arms. Today Lord we ask you to open your loving arms and gather in our children who came to you so soon. May they enjoy being with Jesus and feel his peace in their hearts. Let them know we love them and please keep them safe until we can hold them ourselves.

Amen

Questions

Why did he die?
How did it happen?
When did he leave me?
Where could I have gone wrong?
What should I have done differently?

Why can't I have a funeral?
How am I going to say goodbye?
When can I be allowed to grieve?
Where do other parents go to talk?
What do I say when people want to know?

Why should I be OK?
How am I supposed to move on?
When will I feel like myself again?
Where can I go to find help and support?
What will my life be like, it can't ever be the same

Rainbow Rachel

Rachel is our Rainbow Baby
Our angel here on earth
She came into our lives
A blinding light at her birth

She knows about her brothers
In heaven looking down
She prays to them quite often
And talks about them around town

She won't let me call her baby
Not now she's a grown up girl
But in private she loves nothing better
Than cuddling up in a curl

Life with a rainbow daughter
Is better than I ever thought
I thank God every second
For the joy that she has brought

Saying Goodbye

Families whose babies have died
Need a chance to remember and cry
Now, at last, there will be a place
For them to come and say goodbye

At Cathedrals around the UK
Services are accessible for all
With music and readings and love
You can stand together or let yourself fall

At each service there's a symbolic act
A mark of remembrance with the use of bells
It's not so much about letting them go
But about helping us all to feel well

Don't hesitate, find a service near you
Come along and look to the sky
Together we'll stand side by side
And to our babies we'll say goodbye

Saying Goodbye is part of the Mariposa Trust.
They offer International support and remembrance services for those
who have lost a baby in pregnancy, at birth or in early years.

Tears

Tears are welling in my eyes
Tears of shock, a bad surprise
I can't believe I've had this news
Please forgive my watery ooze
Tears still flowing every day
Tears of baby gone away
When I open each sympathy card
I try to stop, but it's too hard
Tears keep coming now and then
I wonder if it will ever end
Perhaps like grief it'll ease not go
And so these tears will often flow

Unforgettable

Best sung to the tune of "Unforgettable" by Nat King Cole

Unforgettable
That's what you are
Unforgettable
Now you're away so far
That's why baby
It's incredible
That my boys
So unforgettable
Are held in my heart
Unforgettable too

Veil

There's a veil over my eyes
Makes the world duller to see
Where once the sky was blue
Now it's grey to me
There's a veil over my heart
Makes the world seem cruel, unkind
Where once I was full of peace
Now to joy and love I'm blind
There's a veil over my life
Makes everything full of despair
Where once I saw years of hope
Now I give an empty stare
God lifted off the veil
Slowly letting me see
The hope and joy and love
And the life awaiting me

Wailing

How I wish that I could wail
Like African women do
Shout and scream and cry and wail
It'd be better than feeling blue
Getting together with other girls
To share the grief of loss
No longer trapped at home alone
Pretending I'm not sad or cross
In other cultures women know
How to mourn together
I wish we could adopt the same
And be clear it lasts forever

Kisses and Hugs

Kisses and hugs
That's what this means
When online
Communicating by screen
There online
That is where
I'm safe to be me
I really can share
About my grief
The pain I feel
Fall apart
Let it be real
Online friends
Have been to me
True lifesavers
Helping me grieve

You

You will always be in my heart
You will be daily on my mind
You will never be away from me
You are always part of our family
You brought hope into our lives
When you died you know we cried
You were loved and are loved still
You only died because you were ill
You are with your brothers now
Together always playing, wow
Until I join you there one day
Know that I'm not far away

Zipped up grief

My mouth was zipped
I couldn't speak
Society banned
Me to mention grief
But I broke out
I didn't care
I told my story
I had to share
If we all talk
About our grief
Taboos will be broken
It'll bring relief
Unzip your mouths
Share all your tales
Let others know
They can also wail

A baby died; it couldn't be worse

When talking about your loss
Your miscarriage, ectopic or still birth
Being clear is essential to make others know
That "A baby died; it couldn't be worse"

Don't go beating around the bush
To save other people's feelings
Your grief is real, hard and true
Whether old or in it's beginnings

Of course there are those times
When we don't have any energy to share
In that moment just hold on tight
To friends, please don't despair

Together we can make it
Through the dark days and nights
We can lean against each other
And our babies we'll always hold tight

When we need them, there they are

I see glimpses of my boys, in the world in which I walk
I don't think it's possible, but somehow it is
I hear a sound I longed to hear, I see their eyes look at mine
I know that they are giving me, some type of sign

Most days I ignore these signs, push them from my thoughts
But sometimes I focus in, I get the comfort I have sought
Anyone whose baby has died before their time
Knows that they are everywhere, they're always seeking a sign

Rainbow babies, not replacement babies

Some people ask me why I still think about my babies who died before birth. I am constantly shocked that anyone would think this needed to be asked or that anyone would think that the birth of Rachel, my rainbow baby, would make the death of the boys before her go away.

Today is Rachel's sixth birthday; a day of celebration and joy. Yet in the small hours of the night of her birthday I'm always awake, as I was in the hospital the night she was born. I wonder at her life, the miracle of birth and I thank God for her.

I also spend time thinking of my boys who I never held. That might seem like a strange thing to do, but for me it's part of motherhood. I am a mum to five children; four are waiting in heaven.

Rachel is ONE of my children; not a replacement for anyone else. Rachel understands this; she talks about her brothers in heaven.

Sure Rachel's birth helped me heal from my grief; sure her life is the joy of my life. But that will never take away the memory and loss of my boys, her brothers.

Rachel is not a replacement; she's precious in her own right, as are all five of the children who grew within me.

Further Information

Miscarriage Association

If you would like to know more about miscarriage, how to support a grieving family or receive support yourself then please contact The Miscarriage Association. They have a UK-wide network of support volunteers, who have been through the experience of pregnancy loss themselves and can offer real understanding and a listening ear. Most offer support by telephone and some run support groups.

The Miscarriage Association provides support and information to anyone affected by pregnancy loss:

Call them on **01924 200799**
(Monday to Friday, from 9 a.m. to 4 p.m.)

E-mail them at info@miscarriageassociation.org.uk.

Saying Goodbye

Saying Goodbye is part of the Mariposa Trust. They offer International support and remembrance services for those who have lost a baby in pregnancy, at birth or in early years.

www.sayinggoodbye.org

Printed in Great Britain
by Amazon.co.uk, Ltd.,
Marston Gate.